EXODUS IN X MINOR

Sundress Publications • Knoxville, TN

Editor: Erin Elizabeth Smith
erin@sundresspublications.com
http://www.sundresspublications.com

Colophon: This book is set in Georgia.

Cover Art & Design: Trista Dymond

Back Cover Design: Katy Bilbrey

Book Design: Erin Elizabeth Smith

EXODUS IN X MINOR

FOX FRAZIER-FOLEY

Acknowledgments

"For Maddy Lerner, Age 4, Accidentally Killed at an Outdoor Firing Range in Upstate New York" appeared in the summer 2009 issue of *Western Humanities Review*, under a slightly modified title.

"Peter Was One of Four Catholic Workers in Upstate New York Who Spilled His Blood at a Military Recruitment Center in Protest of the USA's Invasion of Iraq, and Was Subsequently Arrested and Imprisoned" appeared in the July 2014 issue of *Luna Luna*.

The fourth poem in the series, "The Fox-Haired Girl Visits a Spiritualist Medium in Upstate New York, and Sees One of Her Past Lives" appeared in the July 2014 issue of *Luna Luna*.

"Gretchen Foggerty, Mother of the Raven-Haired Seer's Friends Philomena and Amelia, Was Arrested for Harassing Father Roderick, Parish Priest, Who Years Later Would Be Arrested on Multiple Charges of Pedophilia and Excommunicated" appeared in the July 2014 issue of *Luna Luna*, and is forthcoming in a print anthology of selected *Luna Luna* authors.

The author gratefully acknowledges the following people and organizations for their kind support of her work: David St. John, Susan McCabe, Mark Irwin, Stacy Gnall, and Elizabeth Cantwell, for providing acute critical feedback and invaluable creative support. Janalynn Bliss, for conversations that stimulated hope & reflection during the time of these poems. The beautiful and amazing Beth Couture, for seeing something in this collection that made her want to share it with others. Trista Dymond, for producing dark and dynamic cover art based upon her experience of these poems. My wonderful Sundress editor, Erin Elizabeth Smith, and all of the Sundress family that welcomed me. My family, especially: John, Norah, Paul, Moog, G, C, Auntie M, and my House. My ancestors, the lwa, and the Numinous.

Table of Contents

We are so hungry food loses its form to sugar and water.
And we can live for a while killing

foxes and roasting them on a spit. In the window of the
abattoir of what-we-can't-give-you

is this scene: the butcher removes the beef heart and lobs
it onto the table, the dark melt pools.
- Ethan Hon

Exodus in X Minor

whiskey-shooting   copperhead   prodigal

newly stripped   needling
bodied   with surreptitious ink   one delicious

brunette bartender mixes all my martinis & Xanax

lets me sleep at last   another, gravel-throated & strawberry
blonde, picks bluegrass after hours   *Won't you*

bury me beneath the tree where my family lies   my family's

scattered below the Mason-Dixon line   parents errant
self-made orphans   who wandered into this overcast vortex

& shipped me yearly home to grandmother's Bittersweet

Farm   haunted by a red-bearded plantation owner who
turned the wrong house slave into a widow *Won't you*

bury me   sleep on the brunette's mattressed floor to hide

from the red-bearded man who hurts me when I
tell him to   sometimes when I don't   ensconced in her

damp comforter   dreams of the night I was 7 and saw him

wandering the halls of the big house with a candle   harmless
     in his white starched nightshirt   I didn't know

                    enough to fear him   There are no

such things as ghosts is something mother
     never told me   *beneath the tree where my family*

          lies father's best friend was stabbed to death

               in front of him last year, one year
     after a gunman stormed the community center of this cloudy town

     and murdered 13 people   The man I'm fucking runs

          his hand over red beard   reading the text
     on his phone   another stripper he used to sell coke to

     is dead from heroin   I think of it as suicide, he says

          he didn't cry   when Kevin's
     skull was split in midtown Manhattan at 3 a.m.

that red-leafed month he left us   *won't you bury me*

     drives to Friendsville, past Quaker Lake, three times
          a week with my dog: rural churchyards, fallen

leaves   streams   occasional blown hay straw   mist   I always

     return   before dark   in truth   I fear   even Quakers *beneath the tree*   the red-bearded ghost

never hurt me   circled myself with salt & wished he would

                         prove himself real   somehow   had nightmares in
which he did
              woke up terrified   satisfied   My father watched his friend

           carried out of his office a corpse, the guilty

           student in handcuffs   knife on the floor   *where*
             *my family lie*s   My father said,   Go to

           sleep, I won't let anything hurt you   Oh my   red-

                   bearded man   holds me
              tightly by   my throat & I

                relax   My red-bearded man cuts me

                 another line   it is dark
by 4 p.m. in this town   *Hear the willow's cries.*

For Maddy Lerner, Age 6, Accidentally Killed at an Outdoor
Firing Range in Upstate New York

Dear Madison, I was told of your death
over dinner. You were, they said, struck

by hot brass from your mother's new
AR-15 with custom scope. A tiny girl

at the table behind ours hit
the lights and the television

glowed in the dim like
when Miss deGrassi turned

off the movie of *Medea*, and there
was a wispy, blue-lidded anchor

saying *Columbine*, school pictures
across the screen. Bryan Andrews

was handing me a piece
of gum. He paused, snorted,

said, *They look like dorks.*
Maddy, when I was your age,

Andy Boyle brought bullets
to show & tell. He got detention

and a beating. The waitress brought
our bangers & mash. My first

trip to London, Clive told us that four
weeks after the preschool episode

in Scotland, all of the handheld kind
were banned. One woman

from New Jersey volunteered, *That would
never work where I'm from,*

and Clive said, *Of course not,
you all think you're cowboys.*

That fall, my friends and I left
daisy wreaths on the armory steps.

When he heard, my ROTC
boyfriend said, *It's the year 2000*

*and there won't be
any more wars. If this*

*is what you think of me,
forget it. Gas is expensive,*

and left me in the rainy lot.
The next morning he filled

my locker with flowers.
Maddy, I'm scared

to ask how they feel
in the meat of you: the shells

fell warm against
my hand & I saved

the target to hang in my fire
escape window that won't lock.

When they asked over dessert
how the first shot felt, I thought

of you & said, *I'd never held
a gun before today*. The souvenir

shell in my purse, I said,
It was great, which felt like

saying, *I'm brave*. Like saying, *I have
nothing to do with this*.

Cachexia collects its echoes:
my sacred cache of chambers.

Breath is hymn. Is He. Vermillion
   cataclysm   walled calligraphy:

refuse silence   flood currency
of speech   These divided reach

for relics   weighed & measured,
wanting   the crude, the stark

the fractured Temple   Insatiable
   scions of sciamachy   I am still

but breathe among these
stirring lions in the dark.

LETTER TO DIANE ARBUS

Some among us are always thumbing absently for the worn

                horn of a saddle in our memory, teeth

           clenched against the cold of that snowful skyline blown so
sleek you can't

      discern river from road.

(Or: dying

              to make love in a wax body

                         museum.)

and the coroner find in my

        cardiac muscle that kernel of

(*singer-sewing contest, soap box derby, eating or drinking (pie watermelon), diaper derby palisades, walkathon St Louis, chess champ, miss appetite, miss fluidless contact lens, yeast raised donut queen, miss peel appeal natl idaho potato week, tooth health week queen, miss press photog, miss antifreeze, miss saltwater taffy wk.*

As a child, I dressed

        one October as a crash

    test dummy.)

The Fox-Haired Girl Visits a Spiritualist Medium in Upstate New York, and Sees One of Her Past Lives

The sweater I will

not finish:
     crossing cables

     to mean married life.
Wet air peels paint

from our ceiling.
     It needs my man's hands.

     Tea without milk.
New wool tangled

in the needles, waiting.
     The sweater he left

     in: moss diamonds
for wealth and success.

Water that rises
     then slams as it

        mixes flesh with
its salt and its depth.

Mast ripped by waves
        from the rest

        of his ship – that first
sweater: cables

ran down it
        like fishing rope.

        Wet air makes
me ache

for our sealing: how I need
        my man's hands.

        Water that boils
before mixing

in the bathtub with
        cold, the waves

        made by a body
easing in.

My grandmother, bed-ridden, bled
from her kidneys, her brain, and the skin
beneath my nails began to blue
chronically. I streamed hot
water over them, transient
fix. We marveled at the bruising
balls of ice our lawn collected, felt
thunder through the porch beams
where we sat watching fire branch
in the sky, Lord, in the sky
and somehow light nothing. Our street
began harvesting mattresses
curbside, our neighbors shielding
their rashed arms & legs, bitten
by insects that moved like apple
seeds tossed in a breeze. I hummed
   will the circle
     be unbroken
under my breath for weeks. I cut
the tips from my gloves, the better
to wear them always. We sipped
our whiskey & the cracked glasses
held. We took a pup the breeder couldn't sell
   by and by, Lord, by and by
we fed her, blanket-wrapped. She nosed
my shoulder until she fell asleep. We woke
to find her dead. We named her

Whiskey. My nails purpled. My red-
bearded man took to the woods for several days
and nights, barrels
loaded for turkey. He returned carrying
nothing but purple
winter roses. *I'll forge you
a blade*, he said. *We'll call it
fox tongue*. He held my
hands in his, and they felt him.

Cousin Magdalene's Husband Burned Down Their Apartment
Building When His Meth Lab Caught Fire, and Her Lover Shot
Himself to Death in Front of Her and Her Three Small Children
Two Months Later

last moments   before you   open the door   know it will

    hurt   children assembled   lover cowering   eyes small dishes whose

low centers have   gathered   loose   drops   It will hurt   this   opening

                your skull with bullets   your heart   won't stop right away

        Tarnish-free   is a promise   you're ready   to cash in on

    three children   clustered   on her lap   she tries   to keep them & they try

        not to move   she might   be speaking   you   are ready

                    to open that door   & not be sorry

    again   her voice   familiar white rush   & just enough   impurity

        enough

                empty   after   in which *the right thing* is a drab damp bundle of twigs that won't light   in the low   center of calm

                                                    the knob in your hand

        is ready to snap shut & open you   open you open

                                                yes yes yes yes yes

you   consumed

                        like a twin

                              in the womb   (Museum

                  it in a bottle: axolotl
                              in formaldehyde, sterile

                        & staring, perilous as a novice
                              bride of Christ).

                sweet anaerobic
                  frenzy   gilded

      point each volant
        contraction

             can't remove

   syntactic fantastic
    synaptic collapse

happy apathy
    slap of apnea

                              tactile epiphany
                                oxidizing lakeful red

more more more more

                red

THE FOX-HAIRED GIRL VISITS A SPIRITUALIST MEDIUM IN UPSTATE NEW YORK, AND SEES ONE OF HER PAST LIVES

When they came to us, I was two and had just died
                    for the first time, ensconced by my river, my father

had caught and breathed me back. I blurred towards his sky
                    colored eyes, the mud-red of his hair. I could see all

the secret threads that web the world. I knew they would
                    come to us hungry. I held my mother when tiny bubbles

of disease devoured her: I knew what she would
                    when swallowed. I sent her with the message of my

hand in hers. I touched the river's bottom. My *sissoh* appeared.
                    My father had known them as a child. We warmed

and fed them. I warmed to one my size: he showed
                    me how they drew their words. They used to call it

alchemy, he said, when metals combine and turn
                    into other metals like magic. I believe it's real. I can

see what the river plans to bring us, I told him.
                    It tells me. We stood in to our ankles. My *sissoh*

watched, contented. The second time I died, by a water
                    snake's bite: he found me gone and carried me

into the long house. I returned that evening. My *sissoh*
                slept beside me as I sweated through night; no one

said a word. I could see every silver thread that bound
                us to who would bring our end. I could see my river

hold us safe for many seasons. I lived to measure time
                in children. My *sissoh* never far. My alchemist observed

my dark hair change to silver. *All I have left*
                is love. Those threads flowed from my body. We had made

our kind of new. My third time, I was ready: *Return me*
                to my river, I asked him. He felt my current slow, placed

his hand in mine. My *sissoh*'s auburn brow. *I'll find you*
                again   *If anyone has a message, tell her now.*

Exodus in X Minor

our streets grew red with men
        painted by vernal cold, behaving
                as ibises   searching

                                        My red-bearded man knew a hill,
                                        one night dug a hole that guided

for serpents, bare-toothed & welcoming
        storm winds   the rivers rising as
                though they meant to come for us

                                        blood into the soft earth.
                                        I woke to find him staring.

and did   the waters browned
        what had been green
        swallowed   one poxed bird

                                        Our sheets a muddied shroud:
                                        The only woman who knows

spread her wings   exposed
        garish plumage   treacly
                feathers gaping   body

                                        me, he said   threw a bottle
                                        of whiskey   my way   chased

sored   floated & eyed
        the red in his beard
                wood piled with bodies

                                                it with wine   screamed, *Get out
                                                of my house*   the doorway

drifted past   the waters moved
        the waters left us   having claimed
                their tithe our steps grew

                                                stained red for weeks   He
                                                dreamed so hard of eyes

red with her: I had
        drawn the blade he forged me
                        and knew it was mine.

                                                that never closed: I saw them
                                                I saw with them.

LETTER TO DIANE ARBUS

Blessed are those

among us able learn a few new

        walls out of all the surrounding

buildings housing strangers: that is to say, bodies

              and the time they give us.

Or: Stepping over purple-eyed

                prostrates, the hotel a kaleidoscope

of verdigris & gangrene.

      Top floor, a bedded

           man cloaked & preening

                    in estrogen
               & negligee ——

she thrashed   she undressed

                                        his rectory room, shirt

by shirt   shoe by shoe

This belt, my girls, keeps me chaste.
Sometimes I do feel the urge. I admit

Your beautiful faces.   Examine

your conscience. The truth: What

have you wanted ––

                                                she flailed, she assaulted

        homily   service   pews   she threw

    her body facedown in the aisle

he strips them in school,
            she sang, dancing backwards.

            Face tilted:
            My child.

                                    Who regarded us? Rapt
                                        captives of pulpit.
                                    Opiated. Apt. Exalted

He said suffer them unto me   he said   I tell you: sow a thought,

reap an action

by fountain & silence   whose festering kindness

Who bled & who learned

of alchemy's black: the sore, the burn,

that Wound plunging deep in the side

rendered whole as stained glass: bright slivers

of feather, of water, of fern
(the bullet implied)

sow an action, reap a habit

whose core cracked

sow a habit, reap a destiny

& brittle as the breast-
          bone of a bittern

these cushions fatten

us: twisting, contorted,

finding

some new
way to become

(weathered, Other)

I mean my coat

of human

My zipper.

Peter Was One of Four Catholic Workers in Upstate NY Who Spilled His Blood at a Military Recruitment Center in Protest of the USA's Invasion of Iraq, and Was Subsequently Arrested and Imprisoned

strangle makes a minute

oubliette   forgetting

is the war

These are waterless springs and mists driven by storm. The greatest darkness has been reserved for them.

soldier's skull halved   like melon & filled   by time with rainwater

I could drink it   I'm a razor blade

now   no aphagia   emulous

timorous   tremulous

The dog laps its own vomit. The sow is bathed only to wallow again in mud. The earth was first formed in

There, there

is Atlantis.

water; the world of that time was deluged with water and perished. The present world
and heavens have

ubiquitous

obsequies

what   fraught

requiem

been reserved for fire. They shall be kept until the day of judgment and destruction of
the godless.

It is Roanoke.

THE FOX-HAIRED GIRL VISITS A SPIRITUALIST MEDIUM IN UPSTATE NEW
YORK, AND SEES ONE OF HER PAST LIVES

        unwed *mari* *maison* *cérulé* tree
        hive heavy with buckwheat honey

siwo myèl
   siwo myèl mwen

           he called it my *Abbaye d'abeilles*

    I called him *mon homme rouge*

       anmorèz mwen   he called me *dantèl* *ti fanatik* his little lace fan

    lit candles & chanted
psalms with bowed head in the night

         his beard glowing red *why don't you light*
                      one for us
                        for me

Et ce que
      l'on pourrait nous demander, chéri? then   came my belly then

      bebe mwen, pitit mwen

I told my bees

Vandredi sen
          weaning began   *dimanche de Pâques*

                    caught   his face

                                        in unsheeted glass

                    cut his teeth hard
                              skirling skyward   so corded
                    brittle   days

     &days   starving
                    full of his spittle

I wept   beneath the hive
   left heaping   star thistle

        donned tiny drops of their nectar
                eat of me   begged him   to live

                            he fastened   esurient
                                insurgent   my hive   his *viviandiére*

                small calcified darts
            forced the skin's final give   he punctured

                                me   his willing intinction   the honey

        that year was dark   sweet tar wine   someday all would be lost & I'd

            bury them   tiny pinked pearls   among its *racines*

                        seventh birthday   bought for his father
                                pearl-handled long-coveted   knife

    yon kouto tankou
       yon kado koupe

nights at the hearth, both darkened by cinders
                    they sat, whittled branches for kindling

ou renmen
     nan anpil grenn

          its handle   in   flame recrudesced

          opalescence   together   tendered

          slender boughs tinder

                         at fifteen, caught & beaten
                              the gashes immeasurably

          obscene   they called him   *vitrelline*
                              citron de maladie

dark red bubbled   the base of my tree
                         46

to heal him   a tincture   blood   honey   *dlo beni*

he spat   resistant to poultice   hissed
talion of the tartuffe

*oui, c'est ce que tu es   how could you
love him   what he made you
made me*

cursed me   & my slim   volar knowledge
I will slice up your roots   I will end your sick tree

his shoveling thrusts breezed against the wrong branch
bees skirled   encircling my churl

I could not cry him back   *pitit mwen
bebe mwen
stay with me   please*

*You'll never see me again
in this life but you will

see me again*

47

on the third day   he shed   honey bandages

left me   for good   chased after   by bees

LETTER TO DIANE ARBUS

Hooked, quick,
          dactylic – he thought he'd found his long
                    pink sleeve in

                    me who could not sane
        herself a stationary

                              sheet set.   Me,   I need to be

It's the sweetest

                        among us whose hides become

acquainted with impressions
                    of heels; we acquiesce to taking

        our quiet where
we can find it: Razor blade learning

                        to unlink the cuffs of the skin

pummeled. As in

parachute wind.

EXODUS IN X MINOR

The bodies piled in our hot cellar:

black-and-yellow pebbles ambering

in the humid air.   I gasped

each time I saw them. Public gardens

closed, parks nursed their suffering

baby oaks as a mother publicly

failing her children. Frogs

stormed our cellar, declaring *one*

by one, we'll gain the portals

with a shock of teeth. I moved

my paintings from our basement

mausoleum. Our tall field's

fireflies never appeared   *there to dwell*

with the immortals   My red-bearded man

sailed the rivers to their confluence on a ram-

shackle raft: it capsized

twice before he finally swam

that land beyond the river, arrived

 home & held me against his nude

Celtic ink: my throat

swelled shut. I wheezed for weeks

at his skin. I took my paintings

from the walls. I learned to squeeze

my blade so that no blood would come.

I held its handle. I rolled my

wrist under its weight. I held

   my breath.   I counted.

Stranded in Rural Upstate New York, the Fox-Haired Girl Walks
Miles to the Nearest Building, A Small Abattoir, Seeking Relief
from the Elements

Her twin waits, throat-splayed,

hapless on the hosed concrete.
        A fresh knife sharpening

jingles, insouciant   Hooks,

pullied,   hang the beauty
higher   as he strips   the canvas-

thick balloon of

hide from the body.
The floor mixes

into marble: her face freed

of its fluids, her eyes
bright as a mime's, naked

legs pieced in graceful

jerks, the skin-
        less wound still

flowing, broochlike, the dark

size of a bauble. The true
belly, already wheel-

barrowed, swells in

this heat. They're known
to explode, these summers,

but no one steps away.

THE FOX-HAIRED GIRL VISITS A SPIRITUALIST MEDIUM IN UPSTATE NEW YORK, AND SEES ONE OF HER PAST LIVES

Who was I to tamper or beg
the swannish fate of Leda? I took

the sieve, watered it, walked across
Rome with it full. It was true,

I had begun to feel my womb
hollow for a daughter. But I

would not suffer her to be buried
with me, our lungs learning dirt.

At times I turn to find the children
whose voices I have heard are

simply certain tones of wind.
The irrefutable tremor of my own

hand delivering these sacred tongues
their unborn calf, milky & still. Who

am I, now, to imagine moments
of convulsion against downy breast, or

the cleaved immortality that comes
after?   And so, beloved,

I take you, he said, and meant I was
perfect, in my seven year-old body: chosen

to tend flame for you, Mother of our
hearth, who know me best – abject

in all but my appetites, smothering
under desire like smoke or wings. I stare

into the gibbous reds and yellows
as they eradicate each other, silent

save the occasional whisper, *I am*.

Even   nascent   bodies
crave   pleasance.   Dreams
 delivered by celestial

fire fall fallow. Soft belly,
not without grace   Crawling,
we learn to rise   where to place

the self like a chalice   in brume
steel-bound wrists   whirling lights like ice
floes before dawn   Immersed: our ceremonial

nerves   in quieted hours   find
     calm   in ascetic   cells
cathedrals   arctic solace   aurora   Polaris

like skyflower   jessamine   we climb
clinging   yet to ground   Through
heather   though esker   solaris

LETTER TO DIANE ARBUS

Less a howl, now,
at the moon than a hat
  brim over the eyes: orange

cylinder spilling pills like sun-
flower seeds into your palm. The flash lost

                              in a series of flashes.

                (yes   you wanted this
                          like tattoos)   Lonely as a dial tone.

Exodus in X Minor

finally sped   West together   letters   that followed us read
    wash out all the violet

        you'd like to   *we remember*   *you when the fire*

gutted downtown   you when a man stormed Main Street

        with samurai sword hacking limbs

    from strangers   you when the gorges

   froze and kept flood waters in our streets   *you*   *when we know we'll*

      disappear   my pocketed fox tongue
      hummed like an extracted
      heart: the thrill

      of cleaving had left me
      wanting more than dove or lamb

or Fox: horizon like sweet cold razing
liquid or a wristed razor. Beyond. Be-
yonder

    we saw aubrenwing lilaced by evening
    we climb like viola strains into the air

        we escaped   we are
            escaping one carved

tree trunk at a time   towards our Croatoan

              not being but becoming

     creatures newer   more brightly made

Notes

"Won't you bury me/ beneath the tree/ where my family lies/ hear the willow cry" is a phrase from the Steeldrivers' song, "Hear the Willow Cry."

"Singer-sewing contest, soap box derby, eating or drinking (pie watermelon), diaper derby palisades, walkathon St Louis, chess champ, miss appetite, miss fluidless contact lens, yeast raised donut queen, miss peel appeal natl idaho potato week, tooth health week queen, miss press photog, miss antifreeze, miss saltwater taffy wk" is a transcription of Diane Arbus's notes to herself about potential future photography projects, recorded in one of her notebooks.

"Sissoh" is the Susquehannock word for "fox."

"Will the circle be unbroken/ by and by, Lord, by and by?/ There's a better home a-waiting/ in the sky, Lord, in the sky" are lines from "Will the Circle Be Unbroken," a Christian hymn written in 1907, later adapted into the bluegrass music tradition for secular performance.

"One by one, we'll gain the portals/ there to dwell with the immortals" and "that land beyond the river" are lines from the Christian hymn "When They Ring The Golden Bells," written in 1887, later adapted into the bluegrass tradition for secular performance.

The third poem in the series, "The Fox-Haired Girl Visits a Spiritualist Medium in Upstate New York, and Sees One of Her Past Lives" mixes English, French, Haitian Kréyol, and Louisiana Kréyol.

"Peter Was One of Four Catholic Workers in Upstate New York Who Spilled His Blood at a Military Recruitment Center to Protest the USA's Invasion of Iraq, and Was Subsequently Arrested and Imprisoned," contains my own paraphrase of the following verses from the *New Oxford Annotated Bible*:

2 Peter 2:17: "These are waterless springs and mists driven by a storm; for them the deepest darkness has been reserved."
2 Peter 2:22: "It has happened to them according to the true proverb, 'The dog turns back to its own vomit,' and 'the sow is washed only to wallow in the mud.'"
2 Peter 3:5-7: "They deliberately ignore this fact, that by the word of God heavens existed long ago and an earth was formed out of water and by means of water, through which the world of that time was deluged with water and perished. But by the same word the present heavens and earth have been reserved for fire, being kept until the day of judgment and destruction of the godless."

"Aubrenwing" is a neologism, naming the space between sea and sky that you can find yourself flying into if you stare at the horizon.

Biographical Note

Fox Frazier-Foley is an initiate of Haitian Vodou who hails from upstate New York and northern Virginia. Her first full-length collection of poems, *The Hydromantic Histories*, was chosen by Chard deNiord as winner of the 2013 Bright Hill Press Poetry Book Prize, and is forthcoming in 2015. She is a Founding Editor and Managing Editor of the Los Angeles-based small press Ricochet Editions, and Editor-Curator of TheThe Infoxicated Corner at TheThe Poetry Blog. She is co-Editor of a forthcoming anthology of American political poetry (Sundress Publications, 2016) and *Among Margins*, an anthology of critical writing on aesthetics (Ricochet Editions, 2016). She is a staff writer and creator of poetry horoscopes for *Luna Luna*. She was graduated Phi Beta Kappa from Binghamton University, received her MFA from Columbia University, and is currently a PhD candidate and Provost's Fellow in the Literature & Creative Writing Department at the University of Southern California.

CPSIA information can be obtained at www.ICGtesting.com
Printed in the USA
LVOW03s0316261214

420374LV00001B/1/P